I0151323

Dramaturgia Ay Ombe I

Comrade, Bliss ain't playing

Dominicanish

Como la una

Josefina Báez

Dramaturgia Ay Ombe I

Comrade, Bliss ain't playing, Dominicanish y Como la una.

Todos los derechos reservados.

Fotos © Giovanni Savino

2014

ISBN: 978-1-882161-24-9

Our dramaturgy, our work, our path is open, inclusive.
A segment of the dialogue.
The page and the stage will craft specific phrasings of
each text. Its staging is informed by the actor's training,
the director's poetry and the braiding of chosen
parallels.
It's reading is the first intimate performance.
Thus, here we start the possible dialogue.

Nuestra dramaturgia, nuestro camino, es abierto e
inclusive.
Un segmento del diálogo.
El universo personal haciendo coro con otros
universos, con ritmos en clave y ritmos atonales.
Lleno, mayormente de lo más cercano.
De lo más manoseado.
Una dramaturgia sin acotaciones. Pues las acciones
posibles se forjarán desde los entrenamientos
personales, de lo cotidiano, desde lo extracotidiano y de
las trenzas que conjuguen su hoy.

Ay Ombe

Comrade, Bliss ain't playing has been my life's
accompanist.
This is the text where I have bounced to-from-back and
forth while developing Performance Autology (PA).
I have played with its words and vice-versa, testing
physical and phrasing exercises.
Its beauty humbles me.
Its vulnerability makes me strong.

Comrade Bliss ain´t playing

¨God, God, God,

I do not know where any member of my

family is. But you do. That comforts me¨.

My mother, Luz María Pérez vda Báez

I am an urban ascetic,

deciding my own temporary

vows and permanent quests;

an urban devotee initiated

right here in Gotham ´s midtown.

I am a nun.

A non-denominational nun.

A nun with benefits.

A nun married to Harmony.

A nun dancing the sacred with secular riffs.

Dressed in dungarees,

tightly hugged by my man.

By my monk. Man. Monk.

Monk. Man. Monk.

By my man…I

I dentity.   I dent it why.

Identity.

A prioritized

feeling that photographs a nation.

Identity. Flagless nation.

Identity. A nation with no flag.

Identity. A mere feeling.

Iden tity. I

Countless I. I I I I.

iperform, idance,

itele, you phone,

ianswer. I I I.

Again, nothing new under the sun.

Nothing new under the moon.

God within is poet.

Goddess within is poet with action.

Is she a performer?

I arrived to one thought.

Induced, deduced, elucidated.

Or at the exact time when the flapping

wings of a butterfly

stopped in a far away land.

The seed and blossom

of my own revolution.

Not sponsored. Not televised.

My own rrrrrrr evolution.

More often than not.

More often than not.

I always wanted to write this phrase:

More often than not.

I wanted to say it:

more often than not.

Since I have many often

and zillion not.

Not. No. Nuts. Nah. No. Knots.

So many knots that I have crafted

A macramé path.

More often than not.

More often than not.

I travel. I travel to

discover more about my

own self,

as any displaced, surviving.

As any traveler, surviving.

I travel to watch what

I watch at home.

I take the trip.

The trip takes me.

I am tripping.

I have visited paradises on earth.

But they were really

paradises on earth

because I was just visiting.

After those visits, I granted

to my life its ¨visiting earth¨

bumper sticker.

Continuing with the tourist itinerary…

if the glossy color photo is scratched a little, it bleeds.

Few local people could swim…

Heaven advertised for the Hereafter…

Please read it as purgatory

lived by the majority,

in this current life.

Look at the eyes of the

smiley-Happy-party people

full of anger.

Hunger.

Anguish.

Sadness.

Countries export what they need.

Saints and sages.

Workers and lovers.

Workers are lovers.

Lovers are workers.

Countries export what they need.

Teachers and doctors.

Spirituality.

Democracy.

Diplomacy.

Artists and scientists.

Flowers and fruits.

Silks and diamonds.

Prayers and magic.

Countries export what they need.

As we teach what we need to learn.

As we look outside what

we already have within.

On the trip…

I'm tripping.

The lowest price package, with all

possible amenities

and national anthems included.

It is impossible to relax in

paradise when you are one

of the supposedly smiley-happy-party people too.

But, when I hear the word

tradition, sorry, I must run

to the other side,

miles and miles away.

Paradises on earth and their… traditions.

I have my own tradition.

I do.

Not colorful, gold

Picture perfect lore.

No beautiful fabrics to die for

or dances to live by

or hips swinging truths or lies.

No.

In my tradition, breathing

is the only expression to keep alive.

And you too can testify for that.

Fake it, fake it, faaake it

and your lungs will react automatically.

This is it. The core.

Now playing at a theatre

so near you that you can't

wait to exhale.

'Cause you will practically die.

I take the trip.

The trip takes me.

Still tripping.

I have been migrating since birth.

In fact, migration

first comes visible exactly at birth.

Migrant. Migrate. Migraine.

Migrant migraine.

Migration rapidly wrapped all my existence.

I move from second to

minutes to hours to days to

weeks to months to years

and years and years.

Migrating every day.

Day to night.

Night to day.

To too many places

I have arrived.

From many places I have left.

Heaven, purgatory or earth,

All ask the same questions...

Where are you from?

I am not able to place your accent.

Where are you from again?

Where on earth is that?

Ohhh the name sounds

So cute-so exotic-so strange

so different than us.

Heaven, purgatory or earth

All ask the same questions...

Where are you from?

When are you leaving?

Where are you going?

Like if a "place" would be the thing.

What about if I tell you that

I am THAT place, coming, staying,

going, to-by-from-on-in

I am that I am.

I have a friend who has Rumi's complete collection:

Every published, recorded, videotaped, filmed verse.

He can even recite many of the poems in the original

and best translated languages.

Even his child's middle name is Rumi.

But he takes no notice of our own Rumi

living in the corner.

He, our Rumi, rhapsodizes in poetry

his homelessness reality.

He swings in the subway poles.

He circles and circles around
fetching and airing his trance.
As a dervish too.
Drunk too.
In his way with and to God.
Too.

I will never know what the
other really thinks, knows or feels.
And vice-versa.
Always vice-versa.
Versa-vice. Vice. Versa.
Then, to know is a futile quest
when we talk about feelings.
Go figure.

I might also have that purple crayon.
Like Harold.
Or I simply opened that door titled potentiality.
Soon as I materialized it,
I was given a second opportunity in all decisions
that I have made.
Surprisingly enough I made the same decisions.

Now, with no doubt, I do not have an ounce of regret.

This instance sweated out all maladies attached to any

'could or should have been'.

At last, I identify the IT in all.

Then, the convent, the street, the church, the party,

the ashram and my home

are all the same.

No need to go anywhere.

Everything is everywhere.

Every time includes all times.

Specially now that I am my best company.

All partitions proved themselves limited.

East and West, with their violent blessing

and decadent wealth.

North and South, king and servant.

So called First, Second or Third world rightly

intoxicated with missing links and stolen rights.

And the overdose of

use-reuse-recycle abuse anguish.

The only birthright inherited here, at the tangent, is

the ability to voice your disagreement.

Although voicing the dispute does not mean any

step towards a decent dialogue,

let alone a solution.

But at least you cannot

be taken for a ride by other marginals

or the owners of the circumference.

You know. And they know that you know.

But really, my hyper-individualism started from my

collective living.

And so my battles from sacred teachings.

Blasphemous? Sacrilegious?

Profane? Offensive?

You must be kidding.

My words, unheard whispers,

do not even fan a mosquito.

Universes keep unfolding

all around me.

There is one in particular

where everything

is as I desire; as I wish.

It is not a state of condensed milk,

maple syrup and molasses

over honey with brown sugar sprinkled on top.

No.

Consciousness is the trigger for reaching,

with total assurance,

this splendid space.

To surrender is the verb used.

A peek on the ocean marveled to evanesce.

And I am the tiniest drop.

Me as part of the mist.

Mist me. Me mist.

That's the least. Mist.

Mist did it. It did mist.

Did it, mist?

What I do in the extremes,

in pain or in pleasure,

tells you mathematically

my equanimity level.

I thought that what lasted more

was truer. But time, as we know it,

can not measure truth.

Time in itself is limited.

Reality is constant.

Reality is what is constant.

What is constant, is Reality.

Then, just my soul lives in reality.

Every. Every.

Every routine is my ritual.

And pure potentiality...

my religion.

If I should tell you one truth.

One.

At least one.

Count on my contradictions.

What does life verify anyway?

Where does the dance of life

move towards anyway?

A divine choreography for the

sake of the moment?

Go figure.

Sundays have their own rhythm.

No matter where on earth you are.

Sundays do not have passports,

visas, flags. Nor site-specific behavior.

Sunday's language is worldwide spoken.

Understood.

And nobody is a Sunday's expert.

When I grow up,

I want to be a Sunday.

To surrender is my only virtue.

And to dwell in it,

my lethal vice.

Me in the midst of uncertainty.

Awesome.

… Speaks volume.

Silence speaks volume.

"Before the real dream.

Before the predicted dream.

Before the lasting dream:

the saliva drooling man".

A title.

I have just seen you in my dreams.

And actively the night was lived.

I had you in my dreams.

What happens now when

my pillow is just a decoration

in the invitation for the night?

Where have you gone lover of mine?

Where are you making your present now?

In another dream?

In another life that quickly disappears?

In another pillow covered by prints?

Prints with too many flowers or too many lines?

My heart, while loving, is still.

Still like that moment before

erasing your number.

When I really knew your number.

And I allowed you to do that number on me.

You knew the alchemy of my present.

So you said.

And I thought you really did.

You said so.

Is knowledge a constant?

Wisdom is.

Does it count when you momentarily forget?

Or when priorities change?

Anyway. It was just a dream.

Neither your dreams nor your saliva are present

on my pillows.

Gladly we all know that

the juice happens, regardless of any company.

Anyway, there is always

a presence in absence

I saw you.

I saw you in the sunset.

I saw you.

I saw you as a sunset.

"The real dream".

Another title.

Crisscrossing in life,

I too had a love once.

A dream of love.

A love dream.

The man of my dream.

It was foretold into minute details.

Past and present lives; likes and dislikes;

favorite poems; favorite food,

beginning, middle and end.

Heads, hands, hearts and hips in sync.

And you know that that's

the most accurate definition of

L O V E.

The H syndrome.

The H effect.

Head-hands-hips and heart in sync.

I should start at the end.

Now that there 's no nostalgia.

The farewell banquet included

artichokes and pomegranates.

Honey and almonds.

Figs and dates.

Jasmine flowers and roses.

He went.

Or I did?

We separated long after
our time was due.
He was just one of my blessings.
The ninety-nine others were
pushed until his grace inhabited every
one of my pores.
And lover's plenitude was permanently
written all over me.
Look.
My love 's tattoo.
At the zenith of our love we separated.
The ninety-nine blessings poured in.
Thirteen years of the most complete-honest love
was predicted.
Lived. Alive. A Life.
Lived.
…poetry at hand and honesty in all actions.
Silence and words had the same weight
as hugs and kisses.

Two different people

dreamt the same dream,

at the same time,

in the same bed.

It happened to us.

It was the omen sketching the goodbye.

Our privacy was tight.

Our love was just for us.

For a limited time only.

The astrologer who predicted

his coming, wrote me a letter about his going.

Or my going?

One dishonest lover for your entire lifetime

or the most absolute, wholesome, honest lover

for thirteen years.

No brainer. No need to wait to decide on new moon.

Right then I told you.

Right now I write,

Just give me thirteen years of the greatest honest love.

The day I met him he asked me if I could

marry him that day.

I told him that I did not

have time but could squeeze him in three days later.

It's a deal.

The squeeze?

The marriage and the squeeze!

In three days we were married.

Sweetly squeezed too.

Artichokes and pomegranates for the marriage banquet.

Dates syrup and rose petals

created the drinks.

Pundit John Coltrane's Ballads,

on repeat mode,

gracing the silences.

Jasmine flowers all over us.

A love contract was drafted:

Honesty above all

Daily physical touch

Loving more than eating

Eating more than fighting.

Smiling and laughing galore.

Please do not speak in your

language when I am upset.

'Cause I will immediately

forget my reasons with your song.

I second that emotion.

Nobody is allowed in our

house-in our bed-in our

vacations-in our poetry.

My books are my books.

You can read them.

And vice-versa.

My music is my music...

Good dreams wake me up with

precise poems.

Pomegranate seeds on

my lover's torso.

Religion versed naked.

Again not a frog, not a prince

but a man.

A man of truth.

Transparency. Joy.

A lover of love.

Your love.

He is your company for the

most quotidian time.

Time before or after the celebration euphoria.

Time before or after departures and tears.

Life time.

Life.

He went…

Or I did?

One can not have all the blessings

at the same time.

One of the finest options

will always be to consciously

decide what one will lack.

I did.

I have more questions than answers.

Doubting without being insecure.

Maturing with laughter.

Getting closer to my own death with open arms.

Priority is just an order,

not an urgency.

No celebrity hints followed.

No televised fad imitated.

So I, we continue…

I ran all the way to the end of the world.

The place where time begins

ends-begins-ends.

And guess whom did I find?

Yes, me.

Me, me, me.

Me at the threshold of the

Event Horizon.

I cannot explain it better than versica.

Today's New moon is blooming

full this early morning.

Today's New moon woke

me up with a song.

The song was sang by many.

Many of us were healed…

by a song.

A political song.

A song of a particular politics.

Artichokes.

Yes, artichokes.

Beyond right, left or center.

The artichoke's politics:

Many leaves on the same stem,

Full devotion to one,

all attention to one at a time.

And always count with an

exquisite heart.

Artichoke's party is my kind

of party dear.

Dear Comrade Bliss.

Comrade Bliss.

Bliss.

Bliss

Comrade.

Dear.

Dear Comrade Bliss

Last summer I was cold

Comrade.

Dear.

Comrade Bliss,

have you danced naked?

I guess you always dance naked.

You ARE bliss.

Your dance dresses you up.

Buttoned and zippered you up.

Comrade Bliss,

I saw a topless bar with your name.

They advertised happy hours.

Of course… happy hours

in the House of Bliss.

No less than happy hours.

Topless top more.

Top Bliss.

Bliss tops.

With best regards…

I remain.

Comrade,

The question that I do not

want an answer to,

I ask it in silence.

Dances that I do not want others to dance,

I dance them in solitude.

Tonight I am going to read a book that does not

use even one asterisk.

But before silence sat in,

a monosyllabic sound was mumbled.

You were already in silence.

I was drowning still in words.

I could not help but smile at myself.

Laugh with myself.

And cry for myself.

I remember the silence out of fear.

Silence of ignorance.

Silence by omission.

Silence by violence.

Silence by anger.

Silence when the memory denied access.

Silence when a mere cold wrapped my chords around.

Silence selected as my own choice.

Silence.

Silence.

Many silences.

Complicity.

Not compromised.

Untouched.

Detached.

All had silences.

And I had all of those silences.

And you came with words

that I did not hear.

That you did not pronounce.

Silence in the midst of all noises.

Silence or the beginning of sound...

You silenced yourself.

You silenced itself.

You silent.

Silence. You.

I could not help but love you.

Adore you.

Or learn your way of loving.

Real loving.

Constant loving.

In silence.

In silence we are one.

One is in silence oneness.

One is.
Is in.
In silence.
Silence Oneness.

One is

is one

one is

is in

in is

is in

in silence

silence in

in silence

silence oneness

oneness silence

silence oneness

One is in silence oneness.

It is so true, in the precise

moment of love,

there is silence.

Love in silence.

Silence in love.

Loving in silence.

In silence…love.

And in silence we are alone.

Alone together too.

Solitude dresses silence up.

And vice-versa.

Up silence dresses solitude,

fact in. Versa-vice. With no virtue.

With no vice. No Woman. No cry.

Always vice-versa.

I never want to lose my silence.

Never.

Words do get in the way.

Specially when talking

about silence.

Obviously.

So many times I have said

that it was my conscience

that talked; that my conscience

led me to decide this or that.

But my conscience reacts

with silence and stillness to all.

To all She reacts with silence.

Pristine silence.

Crafted silence filled with all sounds.

...And Stillness.

Stillness containing all movements.

Was I hearing voices then?

I did.

I heard voices before I met

Silence.

… from Silence I go to…to…to…

My voice.

My voice is full of silences.

Walking hand in hand with you,

Silence...the ordinary eye

does not even notice you,

That's the only reason why they call me

The widow in silence.

Silence 's widow.

And the souls of all widows

dance the epitomy of silence.

Souls in a sole dialogue.

From silence to silence.

In silence I found…

more silence.

Silence…

I cannot describe our bond,

Bliss is the closest.

Silence is the highest art.

The heart of my craft.

The craft of the heart.

Yes, the craft…silence

My words have become
wiser than my deeds.
The only way to balance
this sad affair,
Yes I hear you.
Silence.

This language bestows different syntax every time is published. Its commutative law chisels a unique set, in its unending fractal like development.

Poetic and non-sensical texts tapping into unofficial stories and undocumented history.

Language created by the awareness of the ordinary.

Our *Ish*.

Dominicanish

Enough.

In off,

¨kings and servants depend on **each other**.

There can be no king without a servant

And no servant without a king.

For silk comes out of a worm

Gold out of rocks

Fire from a piece of wood

But have you heard of the friendship of a king?

As you have heard   a gambler that is honest

A snake that forgives   a **passionate** woman

who is calm   an impotent man who is **brave**

A drunk with discrimination.

But then again, how can servants be well?

It is said that the poor, the sick, the dreamers

and the fools **always** go into exile¨." *

Poor, sick, dreamers and fools exile.

But you see

There's no **guarantee.**

There is no guarantee **here, there, anywhere**.

There is La Romana

Here is 107th street ok.

There   forgotten deities

looked at me   recognized me.

In the process they became turmeric yellow

I   jet black.

But no one to blame or complain

but go just go   let go

go slow   go fast   but go.

*from Panchatantra

Hips swing   male or female.

We swing creating our tale.

Male or female   we swing

Side side side   Side side side side

Point turn stop   point turn stop   point turn stop.

Repeated a whisper.

Side   side   side

Whispered a little louder.

Point turn stop

Sing **a song**   sang a song

Sang **a whisper**

The list grows   the list grew

Grows grew growing

Growing smooth soft hard

Growing hard   Sweet memory

Growing soft   sweet passion

Growing up   horizon

Promise everlasting   Each and every day

You are the heaven I need to see.

Let's be real   Let's do the impossible.

Loud colors

On silent faces

Rude dances

On angels faces

Sounds dancing   angels facing loud **silent**

Silence on color faces.

¨Who can tell what detours are ahead?

Another trial? Sure. Another jail?

Maybe.

But if you beat the habit again and kick TV, no jail on

earth can worry you too much.

Tired? You bet. But all that I'll soon forget with

my man¨*

My cat is black.

Black is my color.

Black is   a color.

You

You in a secret   you in a whisper

*From Billie Holiday´s biography

———

You are real   you are constant

You are the top in my priority

In my priority   you are the top

In the top   you are my priority

In my priority   you are the top

Are you the top in my priority?

Top top top   priority

Top top top   priority

Top top **top**.

Top top top   Take take **take**.

Take off every safety pin in your way.

Unleash this starched sari.

Let its prints and colors play wild ragas

foreplaying to the juciest kalankhan.

Wild foreplaying to Kalankhan kalakand

juciest ragas

Kalankhan wild foreplaying to juciest ragas

Juiciest ragas foreplaying to wild Kalankhan

Kalakand Kalankhand

Wild ragas

 I NG   the **sweetest** of actions

Love is like a faucet it turns on and off

Love is like a faucet it turns on and off

On   off off   on on   on on

On…

Glorifying the finest brutality in **blue**

Crooked City.

I pulled the emergency cord.

Fight the power   fight the power   fight it

God bless the child travelin' light

Saraswati travels Ri Durga travels

Ga Surya travels

mapadanisa

sa	ri	ga	ma		pa	da		ni	Sa
Sa	ni	da	pa		ma	ga		ri	sa
sa	ri	sa	ri	sa	ri		ga	ma	
sa	ri	ga	ma		pa	da		ni	Sa
Sa	ni	Sa	ni	Sa	ni		da	pa	
Sa	ni	da	pa		ma	ga		ri	sa

Ajjanta weds Ellora   India moves with modi xerox
Ashoka, Nuclear weds Namaste   Government
approved
Mira weds Khrisna   STD ISD PCO STD ISD PCO
Traffic police Birla supreme Maha Cement
for you with you always
STD ISD PCO STD ISD PCO
Fax to let   best of both world   For hire   please
sound horn   veg. Non veg.
Hotel Fresh tickets   I want my thunder
sariga   mapada nisaga
Surya travels.

"For example you see a rope and think it is a snake.
As soon as you realize that the rope is a rope, your false
perception of a snake stops, and you are no longer
distracted by the fear which it inspired.
Therefore, one who wants to liberate **herself** must
know the nature of the real self and the unreal.
When appearances cannot distract you anymore,
then comes knowledge; then comes complete
discrimination of the real and the unreal.
When the vision of reality comes, the veil of ignorance

is completely removed.

When our false perception is corrected, our misery
ends¨. *

Sa ni da pa ma ga, ri sa ni

My king of contradictions,

that verbal addict.

Monolingual linear **lover**.

Crooked cupid

Thanks to the Ganga, Bengal tigers don't move me

long gone tantric attacks.

Let's go to the house of the Lord.

But you see, there's no guarantee.

There's no guarantee

without accent, PhD, CEO.

Now I'm another person.

*From Shri Adi Sankara´s Crest Jewel of Discrimination

———

44

Chewing English

and spitting Spanish.

Mouth twisted

Güiri güiri on dreams

Güiri güiri business.

Even laughing   laughing in Dominicanish.

Yesterday in homeroom and today in the cafeteria,

the bilingual students me cortaron los ojos.

They looked at me with the who-you-think-you-are-

bitch attitude. And the North Americans laughed at my

corny vocabulary.

I ain't no bilingual nerd.

I'm just immersed in the **poetry** of the senses.

Poetry that leads to acts of **love.**

Like **a prayer**.

Like **fore playing**,

SAT scores doubled but in no university catalog

I found my teachers.

I did not see no class, department, major, minor,

sororities, fraternities groovin' with **soul**.

Mister Juarez, My ESL teacher and later Mrs.Kisinsky, my monolingual teacher were amazed, 'cause I had the vocabulary found in wet **tongues** and hooky party goers.

And I, believe it or not, was none of the above.

Me, the Dominican miracle in 84th street

 in Brandeis representin'

Writing phrases and sentences in perfect syntax.

Filled and full of sensual images.

Higher Education took me to places of pain

and **pleasure**.

History in black and white.

I went back there on vacation.

There is La Romana

Here is 107th street ok.

Home is where theatre is

Tú sabes inglés?

¡Ay habla **un chin** para nosotros ver si tu sabes!

Com fortable comfor table comfort able

Wednesday sursdei zerdeis

Every sin' is vegetable.

Vegetable   vegetable

Refrigerator refrigerator fridge.

Son sin' something sin.

I was changed.

They were changed.

 He she it were changed too.

Ando cantando   ING singing

Preterito pluscuamperfecto indicativo imperativo

A **as in** Michael

M as in apple.

Back home   home is 107 ok

Full fridge   full of **morisoñando** con Minute Maid.

To die dreaming as a maid in a minute.

Tu sabes ingles?

Englishsssh ssssh ishsssh

Don't get me wrong   Yo se **un chin.**

I thought that I will never learn English.

No way I will not put my mouth like that.

No way   jamás ni never no way.

Gosh to pronounce one little phrase one must
become another person with the mouth all twisted.
Yo no voy a poner la boca así como un guante.
Me da vergüenza poner la boca **así**.

In a cloud of smoke I found my teachers.
In an LP jacket I found my teachers.
Stiched suede   bell bottoms on.
Openly displaying their horoscope signs.
Gemini Capricorn Pisces **Leo lio**.
In that cover I found my teachers.
Los hermanos Tonga Isley.
Los hermanos Isley.
The Isley Brothers.

Distinguished teachers: Pearl Bailey, Earth Fantasy,
wind September, Reasons and Fire.
Ella Fitzgerald, Louis Armstrong and the dearest
of all, my favorite Ms. Billie Holiday.
Teaching me the ups and downs **of the heart**.
The other side of love.

Last Saturday my teachers sang in Soul Train.

 Drifted on a memory…

 well three times   **Well Well Well.**

No, no, no Samantha Ronald is the cutest

and then Marvin.

Now I'm part of my teachers' tour.

Smoke and all   the Garden.

Smoke and all   the Apollo.

Smoke and all   the Great Hall in San Francisco.

Boy girl loves you   Me Tarzan   You Jane

You me mine   love you do   does and doesn't

Been very very very good to Me Mine Myself.

Myself   frequent flying to the dictionary

grooving it

diggin' it

Perfect   Regular   irregular

Now I don't care how my mouth look

I like what I'm saying.

Boy girl loves you   She does   She doesn't

A mor And more, Add more.

Boy girl loves you   She did she does she will

Chi tu chi sa chi be   chi mu chi cho

!Que bien!

Ain't no place I'd rather be than with you

Yeah

loving you well three times

Well Well Well.

Past perfect   Perfect past.

Past is not present   You know better than anybody

else how **I** used to die to sing like Fausto Rey

but past is not present.

El present is a gift.

Cool as a cucumber   like Peter thru his house

leather leather lederisima   tell me with who are

you hangin' out and I will tell you who you are.

Por h o por R that doesn't ring a bell.

Out of the woods   just out of the boat

with two left feet.

Brujo haitiano brujo Colombiano Brujo de las matas.

Thanks to the Ganga   Gracias al Ganjes

los tígeres de Bengala

no enchinchan la sed.

El salto del tígere hace rato que no es tántrico.

Julio, te quiero mucho pero no tanto para morir por ti

Julio, I love you so much but not enough to die for you.

Marisol   tú no entiendes tú no me quieres **ejmaj** tú

nunca me has querido.

Marisol   you don't understand   you don't love me

in fact, you have never loved me.

Julio mi amor, don't say that, remember what happened

to Anita Rosa Raúl and now Lourdes in decisiones

1, 2, 3, 4, 5, 6, 7, 8, 9*

18   187   781 718 201 212 202 809 1800 646

1 o 2   2 0 1

Although zip coded batey

Water Con Edison galore

Aquí también los pantis se tienden en el baño.

Suerte que la 107 **se arrulla** con Pacheco.

Pacheco tumbao añejo.

*From a public ad campaign about AIDS.

NYC Health Dept.

Pacheco flauta   Pacheco su nuevo tumbao .

El maestro   el artista   Tremendo Cache

compartido en Cruz.

Juntos de nuevo como al detalle   Tres de Café y dos

de azucar.

Con el swing del tumbao   me **chulié** en el hall.

Me chulié en el hall Yo si yo me chulié en el hall.

Reculando como Ciguapa.

Me chulié en el hall.

Metí mano en el rufo.

Me chulié en el hall.

Salgo con mi ex.

Me **chulié** en el hall.

Hablo con el muchacho que estaba preso.

Jangueo con el pájaro del barrio.

Craqueo chicle como Shameka Brown.

Hablo como Boricua

y me peino como Morena.

La viejita de abajo no e' viejita ná.

El super se está tirando a la culona del 5to piso.

Me junto con la muchacha que salió preña.

Garabatié paredes y trenes.

I pulled the emergency cord.

Me **chulié** en el hall.

La lista crece   La lista creció.

Aquí los discos traen un cancionero.

Discos del alma con afro.

Con afro   black is beautiful.

Rooms for rent   GED ESL free classes.

GED ESL Citizenship classes.

Smoke shop 24 hours   calls 39 cents a minute

3 cajas o dos drones   flores para mamá

de aquí allá en minutos

Pasajes para navidad   envios paquetes remesas

haga su casa alla para que la viva el wachiman.

Los suyos siempre presente. Usted el ausente.

El show de los enamorados-de los padres-de las

madres-de las secretarias. El show de navidad-de

independencia-de Semana Santa-de siempre

El show de la risa-de los clasicos del merengue-de los

boleros viejos-del nuevo mambo. El show de siempre.

Phone cards Nuestro canto con viva emoción.

Frituras delivery- a la guerra a morir se lanzó.

Beauty parlor   Dominican beauty parlor

Dominican blowout. Dominican.

Presente y pasado **simple**.

Crece   creció   creciendo.

One way to Santo Domingo

Exchange   today   12.50

Today exchange 33.50

Today exchange 43.75

Quisqueyanos valientes   trips to the airport.

Rest **in peace**.

Balaguer leave us the fuck alone   leave us alone man

leave Me alone.

Dominican cake **any occasion**

march to take back our streets

march against police brutality.

Quisqueyanas valientes celebrando   Abril .

Translations.

An' da' si

But first of all baseball has been very good to me.

Baseball is very good.

Very very good

Very good.

Good.

Baseball has been very very very good to me.

I have been very good to baseball too.

Special signs   signs of specials

donde Roy Foodurama o el 10 cent

Gimbels o Korbette

10 for 1.99   and free with purchase

Pay for it   it's free.

Alexander the Grape   whach you ma' call it.

Repeat after me   whach you ma' call it.

Whach you ma' call it,

If you want to be prompted in English

press one.

If you want to be prompted in Spanish

press two.

Enter your card number.

To place a domestic but not a national call

dial 809.

Todos los circuitos están cerrados

trate su llamada luego   1 kk.

Please leave your message at the   sound of the beep

Gu nai   naigu.

Como la una

Hermana gemela de "Comrade, Bliss ain't playing"
(Canto de plenitud), Como la Una se viste del canto del
alma.
Su poesía incluye cuentos de siempre, compartidos hoy.
Su soliloquio está basado en lo vital y extraordinario,
de lo posíble y cotidiano.

Como la una

Como quiera hablan.
Como quiera dicen.
"La madre, la hija y el burro".
Hay un solazo, un sol que pica.
La hija va al lado de la madre y la madre va al lado del
burro.
Hay solazo, un sol que pica.
Ellas caminan, caminan, caminan, caminan.
El burro trota. Los tres con la rapidez del domingo.
Hay un solazo, un sol que pica.
Quienes las ven les gritan: "Las mujeres no usan la

cabeza. Llevan el burro como arete, lo tienen de biqüi. ¡Qué bobas!"

Se suben las dos al burro.

"Van a explotar a ese pobre animal, abusadoras.

Las mujeres si son abusadoras"

La hija se queda en el lomo del burro.

La madre camina al lado.

Los que critican y no mantienen, pitan y repitan para hacerse notar y anotar el consejo no pedido: "Esa mujer no sabe criar; esa mai no le está enseñando a esa hija a ser considerada con los mayores, después le pesará, después se quejará".

Hay un solazo. Un sol que pica.

Ahora la madre va en el burro y la hija camina a su lado.

Y no son ni uno ni dos, los que vocean la supuesta cachaza de la madre, el infanticidio. "¿Qué clase de mai e' esa?"

Hay un solazo. Un sol que pica.

La madre, la hija y el burro siguen caminando.

Hay un sol. Un sol. Un sol que pica.

Como quiera hablan. Como quiera dicen.

Cuando nací, un conocido dijo:

"Hembra. ¡Qué pena!"

¿Usted haya?   Contesté.

Esa misma tarde pedían a todos los nacidos del mes de enero a ser registrados para un experimento dudoso y no necesario.

Solo a los varones.

El mismo conocido decía en la noche

"¡Que suerte tiene la muchachita!

Nació como la auyama"

¿Usted haya?

Crecía. Crecía con una flor de auyama también en la cabeza, que alegraba a los muchos moñitos que me hacían en mis cabellos.

"Si no fuera por esos cabellos tan 'malo', fuera una negrita bonita".

Ataca de nuevo el conocido.

¿Usted haya?

En mis días y en mis noches mis cabellos crespos, al natural y sin maldad ninguna, no añaden ni quitan belleza.

Así me casé.

"Felicitaciones. ¡Qué bueno!" me dice el conocido.

¿Usted haya?

No tendré hijos.   "Ay, eso sí que es una calamidad"

¿Usted haya?

O moría en el parto o a los 18 años el hijo me mataba
con la indiferencia, con la violencia de su juventud o los
mandamientos de sus tiempos.

Me divorcie.

"¡Qué pena! El matrimonio hay que mantenerlo a toda
costa".

De quien me divorcié era mentiroso, irresponsable e
infiel.

Entonces.   ¿Usted haya?

Entendí.

Entendiste.

Si es que en verdad entendemos…

entendemos diferente.

La decisión estaba siempre posándose en el teorema de
Godel y en el efecto de la mariposa. Entre un sistema
completo pero inconsistente. O uno incompleto pero

constante. Preferí lo incompleto.

Preferí lo constante.

Cierto que una mariposa que bailaba en Pengosekan,

Bali, ayudaba a mi reflexión; al ritmo vital en los pasos

de mi baile.

Yo bailando aquí en Nueva York.

Yo bailando allá en La Romana.

Yo bailando.

Yo.

Conversando con el cielo,

volaba de un batey a otro.

Confirmaba mis pasos en el camino.

Algo que no hice me concedió la experiencia que no da

recuerdos. Que no se queda en el pasado.

Viaje sin mañana. Viaje sin ayer.

Algo que hice me evitó tus límites.

Tus miedos.

Todas las cosas han seguido igual.

Yo,

yo me estoy transformando.

Esta parte de la historia se la oí a mi Gurú.

Estaba un Maestro en las orillas de un río.

Vio que un escorpión se estaba ahogando.

Con su mano izquierda lo llevó a la orilla.

En el camino a la orilla el escorpión le picó.

La sorpresa y la molestia de la picadura a la mano hacen
que el escorpión caiga, sin lastimarse, en la orilla.

Y vuelve al río. Y vuelve a casi ahogarse. Y vuelve el
Maestro a salvarlo.

Y él vuelve y le pica. Y vuelve a la orilla.

Y vuelve a casi ahogarse. Y vuelve el Maestro a salvarle.

Esto se repitió muchas veces.

Tantas veces que el mismo tiempo se detuvo a
contemplar lo que ocurría.

Así lo hicieron también otros seres que no se ven.

El sol, la luna ylas estrellas también .

Un alumno del Maestro, ya molesto de ver la reacción
del escorpión, le preguntó al Maestro que por que
seguía tratando en vano de salvar a esa criatura con
ponzoña.

"Picar es su naturaleza. La mía es amar".

Si digo algo extra, hablaría de más.

De todas formas, si no juego, el juego no existe.

Así de fácil. Así de contundente.

Lo mismo que le pasaba a la abuela Cherokee

me pasaba a mí.

La fuerza interna en su juego de dualidad, multiplicaba

su naturaleza en los adentros. En los afueras.

El jueguito de la dualidad dividió al océano.

Bifurcó las aguas.

Entonces, había dos lobos dentro de mí en plena lucha.

Uno negativo con estos apodos: Envidia, rabia, pena,

lamento, deseos, codicia, arrogancia, culpa,

resentimiento, mentiras, falso orgullo, complejos de

inferioridad, complejos de superioridad,

ego, miedos.

Y el positivo alias: alegría, armonía, paz, amor,

serenidad, humildad, bondad, benevolencia,

generosidad, verdad, compasión, fe,

silencio, plenitud.

Mi hija me preguntaba que quién ganaba.

Cielísima mía, miel de mis días, mi bien, prenda azul,

Susú, solo ganó, gana y ganará al que

alimenté, alimento y alimentaré.

Simple.

Presentes, pasados, futuros… simples.

Simple y sencillamente solo gana a quien nutro.

Vive solo a quien alimento.

Solo existe a quien le doy vida.

La inmensidad que es adentro, para ejercitarla afuera es

trabajo de jardineros, cosmonautas, poetas, artesanos y

ascetas.

Todos en un ser.

Todos en esa sola búsqueda.

Ando cursi.

Entregá.

Llegando a la nada.

Así teniéndolo todo.

A veces lo mejor de mí saca lo peor de los otros

Así parece   así perezco.

No siempre lo peor de afuera, saca lo mejor de mis

adentros.

Delante de mí amamantaron a los pequeños con las frustraciones, no solo de sus padres,
sino de toda la familia, las del barrio, las del pueblo,
las del país, las de todo el continente.
Y ya el pequeño traía las suyas.
Y se rebelaba. Y se revelaba.
Pero no solo con vomitar y eruptar se saca ese tipo de veneno. Entonces le toma tooooooda la vida buscar
de dónde vino, a qué vino y a dónde va.
Nos toma toda la vida.
Se le va la vida antes de sanarse.
Se nos va la vida.
No queda tiempo para la búsqueda vital.
Muriendo en cada intento.
Viviendo haciendo lo que no decidió.

¿Quién ha decidido por mí lo que quiero?
¿Mis gustos?
¿Quién?
¿Qué creó mi discernimiento?

Sería muy fácil encontrarlo todo en un libro, en la
moda, en la familia, en unas vacaciones, en un solo país,
en una religión, en una sola vida.
Sería muy fácil tomarse solo una pastilla y curarse.
Bañarse y realmente limpiarse.
No solamente fácil. Sería imposíble.

Y dentro, muy adentro…
Una palabra abrocha el cinturón para evitar que las
turbulencias sean accidentes fatales.
Todas las otras, son ojos de ciclón o ráfagas de
huracanes.
Hijos naturales de desastres ambientales.
La misma palabra agrupa la sinfonía necesaria
de caminos hacia sí.

Prendo en vida todas las velas de mi muerte.
Todas las flores para esta anima, ya han adornado mi
cuerpo y mi hogar.

Salí a tu encuentro.
Para entretener por un momento la soledad.
Necesito pocas horas de tu compañía para poder seguir

sin ti.

Hago mía tu tibieza.

Juego a las escondidas conmigo misma.

Reencontrandote.

En esas pocas horas del tú y yo.

Universos en cada instantes.

Descubro lunas de tres colores en la habitación.

Amanece y atardece.

Los colores del cielo también entraron a la habitación.

Estos universos siguen multiplicándose.

Sonríen todas las fibras de tu alma.

Encandilando tus ojos.

Co-alquimista de esta intimidad que se abraza de
pétalos y sudores.

La devoción a cada segundo hace que ningún tercero
sea comensal invitado.

¿Será apropiado decirte las gracias hombre miel?

Reniego solo por ocio lo que tengo en el riñón.

El alma me recuerda vestirme solo con delinearme los
ojos con el carbón más negro.

Ahora parecen almendritas.

Sí, en mis ojos aparecen almendritas.

Así que me vestí con dibujar un par de almendritas.

Así…Salí de tu encuentro al sol.

Amor de lejos…

Amor de

tres.

Amor de cuatro.

Hoy quise cocinar algo que nunca había cocinado;
comer algo que nunca había comido y oír las canciones
que me sé de memoria.

Conseguí una canción que nunca había escuchado.

Y preparé los vegetales de siempre de forma diferente.

Todo o casi todo lo que me dijeron fue mentira.

Solo repeticiones de las repeticiones de otra

repeticiones.

Llenas de la ausencia de vivencia de esos credos.

Repeticiones vacías.

Interiores del tambor.

Repeticiones en automático.

Repeticiones de botella.

Mucho de lo que me enseñaron no se aplica.

No tomaron nunca en consideración

mi pequeñísima historia personal.

Todo lo que experimenté me enseñó mis limitaciones y

mis grandes posibilidades.

No hay queja.

No hubo   ni hay   quizás ni habrá un problema en mi

casa que no se pudo evitar con el silencio.

No hubo   ni hay ni habrá un problema en mi casa que

no se pueda evitar con el silencio.

Se pudo evitar con el silencio.

Sí. Se puede.

El silencio que no se deja acompañar del sarcasmo

hecho canción.

Ni un silencio que remenea los ojos y baña de ácido al

pensamiento.

Mi silencio no es ese dedo que quiere tapar al sol.

Es ese dedo que lentamente dibuja al sol en los

contornos de los adentros.

Surce las complejidades.

Borda, juega, salta en punto de cruz.

Primero mostrándome las cadenetas de mi

responsabilidad en el hecho.

Sí, sí, sí las polaridades se tejen en el silencio.

La artesana es la que habla.

Sin obviarlas. Sin abusarlas.

Deshilachando todo el género.

Sus patrones como laberintos.

Sus diseños con toda la gama de colores, sabores, olores, dolores.

Flores.

Con o sin espinas.

Dolores.

Flores.

Convento con flores.

Las mías.

Deshojadas solo por un suspiro.

El mío.

Convento sin flores.

Justo el mío.

Recalcándome mi siempre complicidad en cada hecho.

Dicho.

Hecho.

Por esta quien suspiró.

Por este quien suspiro.

Gimiendo. Sin llorar.

En ningún valle de lágrimas.

Justo en una esquina del laberinto.

Justo ahí.

Abogada nuestra.

Justo juez.

En este destierro de nuestro tiempo.

A otro idioma.

Lugar.

Con otro tiempo.

Justo.

Justo en otro tiempo.

Justo sastre.

En el afamado libre albedrío.

Sigo caminando en vida acompañada del batallón de mis muertos.

En vida muriéndome.

Ellos muertos en vida eterna.

Hasta un día.

Ni antes ni después.

Hasta un día.

Este día.

En el umbral de ilusión y verdad.

Mis hijos hoy lloran mi muerte.

No se dan cuenta todavía de que hoy en verdad nacen a sus vidas.

Hoy que hablo y no me oyen.

Hoy.

Yo serena, en capilla ardiente.

Antes de arder y llegar rápido a cenizas.

Hoy.

Mi muerte abre para mis hijos el horizonte de par en par.

Yo que he estado con ellos desde otros tiempos.

Sigo con ellos.

Ellos sin entender los tiempos.

Los tiempos hechos ciclos.

Tiempos cortados en migajas.

De nuevo.

Tiempo que después del tiempo
desvela aún más tiempo.

Amaron cortándose sus alas.

Amaron viendo por mis ojos. Dejándose enredar por espejos y reflejos de un llamado amor.

Un llamado respeto.

Una llamada responsabilidad.

Que me quitó a mí de mí.

Y a ellos de ellos mismos.

Hoy serena lo palpo.

Hoy.

Aquí horizontal, me desdoblo verticalmente.

No hay forma de alterar el bucle.

"ternura y afan, dulce canto, regazo santo".

Reconozco que así fue mas fácil.

La corriente te lleva desde ayer hasta hoy.

Si me descuido, me regresa de nuevo
al mencionado bucle.

Las tarjetas ya imprimieron lo que supuestamente hay
que decir de pésame.

Solo aquí estando horizontalmente se concretizan las
dudas.

Ver la vida así, hecha toda razón, es de muerte.

Lo inevitable, el mismo horizonte, espera siempre su
tiempo.

Entrega a cada hijo su propio ciclo.

En pleno ejercicio de mi seguro de vida, muero.

Solo seguro la muerte.

Muero tranquila de que nunca exigí devoción.

Muero sin masticar culpabilidad alguna por haber usado verbo de diosa y tomado toda la licencia y beneficios correspondientes.

Ayer era mala. Machorra. Mala madre.

Hoy ni mala ni madre ni nada.

Nada.

Lloran.

Mira, lloran.

Lloran y no saben por qué.

En verdad lloran porque la excusa madre,

la excusa padre perece.

Entonces sin remedio entran oficialmente al Siempre.

Y todo gozo es equiparado por su responsabilidad correspondiente.

Sin yo poder ser más quien desvíe la parte más aguda de la flecha.

Era hoy, dia de mi muerte, que menos queria compañia.

Cuando se acompañan los otros.

Sus sentimientos.

Sus miedos. Sus remordimientos.

Hoy con todos aquí,

Hoy, por estar todos aquí,

se me hará más difícil la primera noche de muerte.

En esa soledad sin espera ni seguridad de nadie.

En el Siempre,

antes y después de la vida.

Otra vida.

Donde yo soy tú. Sin dualidad.

La misma dualidad que nos dejó experimentar el juego

aquí.

Agradecida con la oportunidad.

Pero aquí ya paré.

El juego en verdad es lo mismo con más de lo mismo.

Entretenido. Pero más de lo mismo.

Diferente cada dia. En el corral de lo mismo.

Me voy y me quedo en el siempre.

Sin buscar inmortalidad.

La mirada en el después es tardía.

Innecesaria.

Sobra.

En el siempre somos uno.

Entonces,

es cierto, siempre estamos solos.

Hoy.

En la muerte que creen ver.

Hoy,

que se pertenecen a sus vidas.

Mis hijos.

Hoy sin excusas,

a pesar del gran amor.

Se vive tanto desde la muerte.

En el umbral de diferentes realidades

pauso y no recuerdo nada.

Ya la memoria cedió el turno a su gran posibilidad.

Aquí descubro cada segundo, como primero.

Extraordinario.

Como mismo es abajo es arriba.

Extraordinario caminar sin el piso acostumbrado.

Son tantos los mundos paralelos.

Saqué a pasear a las huellas de las decisiones menores.

O a las decisiones mayores hechas con visión pequeña.

Cierra las piernas.

Eres mujer

Los ecos de las cosquillas son permanentes.

Es que definitivamente lo orgásmico tiene lo cósmico.

Aquí me tienes

zambullida en el presente.

Satisfecha.

Sé de los límites del tiempo.

Del espacio.

Después del límite que creí saber,

encuentro más tiempo,

más espacio.

Sé que todo ha sido mi deseo.

Sé que todo lo he creado.

El deseo solo genera otro deseo.

Cadenitas dulces que engendran cadenitas amargas.

Algunas veces intercaladas.

Una dulce. Una amarga. Una dulce. Una amarga.

Otras veces

Dulce. Dulce. Dulce.

Amarga. Amarga. Amarga.

Como si fuera por racha.

Pero siempre la misma cantidad.

Exactamente la misma cantidad.

La cantidad precisa de todos los juegos de polaridad.

Lo creado dibuja sus otros tantos tentáculos.

Divariando, para confundir al amigo.

Al amigo que es uno mismo.

Divariando, confundiendo al enemigo.

Al enemigo que es uno mismo.

Así me he entretenido en el tiempo.

Sí de nuevo, el tiempo.

Me he entretenido fuera del silencio.

Entre realidades de vidas fugaces.

Entre soledades.

Entre pensamientos.

Entre vacíos.

Acabando también estoy con el tiempo.

Mi tiempo.

Para entrar en otro tiempo.

A otro tempo.

Caminando con la luz en el túnel.

El túnel no tiene final.

Seguimos.

Hoy.

Mañana.

Pasado mañana.

Siempre el mañana es en mayúsculas

cuando se convierte en el Hoy.

Solo cuando llega a su hoy.

Hoy

También…

Abro las piernas.

Soy mujer.

La realidad me arropa hasta durmiendo.

Transita su belleza colándose por las hendijas de los

poros.

Haciéndose sudor.

Haciéndose parte del aura.

Quedándose en el aura

Tocándome el alma.

Verme la mano me despertará del sueño.

Llámenme por el nombre que solo sabe quien me ama.

No, no es el apodo. No.

El nombre por amor. El nombre con amor.

El nombre amor.

El nombre con que me agazaja en medio

de la quietud.

El nombre del bautizo que da permiso para jugetear en el Jardin Perfumado.

Creo que solo él sabe éste nombre.

Creo que quizás no lo reconozco si no lo oigo en su voz.

Trata.

Trata.

Él.

Tú.

Tú eres otro él.

Yo soy tú.

Tú tienes su misma canción.

Mi canción.

El chiste debe ser que solo hay una sola canción.

Y nos creemos autores exclusivo

de la canción que en verdad es de todos.

Por eso te dije.

Somos todos más de lo mismo.

Creyendonos únicos.

Lo único solo estriba

en los niveles ascendentes de entrega.

Otorgados solo en el ámbito de la más alta de las consciencias.

La cura esta siempre muy cerca.

Cerca, cerca. Cerquita.

Mi mamá repite lo que según ella, dijo Jesús.

Es que llamaron a Jesús a revivir a un muerto. Al entrar a la casa lo primero que dijo fue: ¿muerto aquí y salvia en la puerta?

Plenitud del vacío.

Espacio del tiempo.

Más allá del tiempo.

Después de las fronteras del último espacio.

Horizonte de los hechos.

Allá en Versica.

En la quietud.

Principio y fin.

Egoísta y honesta
Preferible a
Generosa y mentirosa.

Si todo fuera como con el café.

No hubieran problemas.

Si está muy amargo se le echa azúcar.

Y si está muy dulce se le echa mas café.*

El silencio de adentro todavía tiene muchos ecos.

Se queda en el dintel entreteniendo mi espera.

La misma muerte es un decir.

Si al final, nunca hemos nacido.

Hoy.

Soy el baile.

Música.

Bailadora.

Yo.

* De mi mamá, Luz María Pérez vda Báez

Josefina Báez (La Romana, Dominican Republic/New York). Storyteller, performer, writer, theatre director, educator. Founder and director of Ay Ombe Theatre (April 1986). Alchemist of artistic/creative life process, Performance Autology© (creative process based on the autobiography and wellness of the doer). Books published: Dominicanish, Comrade, Bliss ain´t playing, Dramaturgia I & II, Como la Una/Como Uma, Levente no. Yolayorkdominicanyork, De Levente. 4 textos para teatro performance, Canto de Plenitud, Latin In and Why is my name Marysol? (a children's book).

Josefina Báez (La Romana, Republica Dominicana/New York). Escritora, performera, directora de teatro, educadora. Fundadora y directora de Ay Ombe Theatre (abril 1986). Alquimista del proceso de creativo/proceso de vida, Autologia del Performance (proceso creativo basado en la autobiografia y bienestar del hacedor). Libros publicados: Dominicanish, Comrade, bliss ain't playing, Como la una/Como uma, Levente no. Yolayorkdominicanyork, De Levente. 4 textos para teatro performance, Canto de Plenitud, Latin In y ¿Por que mi nombre es Marysol? (cuento para niñ@s).

www.ingramcontent.com/pod-product-compliance
Lightning Source LLC
La Vergne TN
LVHW051606080426
835510LV00020B/3150